ANALYSIS

of Ed Yong's
I CONTAIN
MULTITUDES

The Microbes Within Us and a
Grander View of Life

by SUMOREADS

TABLE OF CONTENTS

EXECUTIVE SUMMARY

In his book *I Contain Multitudes: The Microbes Within Us and A Grander View of Life*, Ed Yong goes in search of the invisible microorganism life that occupies virtually every space on Earth. Yong details the complex relationship between large organisms and microbes, observing that every animal is an "ecosystem with legs."

I Contain Multitudes paints the picture of microbes as unsung heroes—behind-the-scenes directors who have steered life for most of Earth's 4.5-billion-year history. From being the common ancestors of plants and animals to commandeering the evolution of species, microbes have always been there, unnoticed, until they were first observed by a Dutch city official in the 1670s. Yong narrates how the conflicting relationship between microbes and their hosts continues to unfold today and how scientists are beginning to repurpose bacteria to enhance the life of their hosts.

Yong sees microbes as both parasites and partners, playing multiple roles from directing the development of organisms to influencing their behavior. Microbes, he observes, are not inherently good or bad; many species can be both beneficial and harmful depending on context. He calls for a multi-pronged approach to treating conditions that involve microbes because these microscopic organisms live in delicate ecosystems, the destruction of which leaves the body susceptible to pathogens.

EDITORIAL REVIEW

Long before Antony van Leeuwenhoek first used his microscope to observe tiny, slithering organisms in lake water in the 1670s, a few dilettantes had speculated over the possibility of unseen life in water and air. Jain scriptures, from an ancient Indian religion, had described the existence of microbial life in 6th century BC, as had Roman scholars in 1st century BC. But in the absence of microscopes—whose development was still centuries away—these unproven guesses collected dust on the shelf of ideas ahead of their time.

Enter Leeuwenhoek and his makeshift microscopes in 1673, and the world was opened up to another thriving world beneath what was visible. The young microscopist, who had never been trained as a scientist, described "tiny dancing animalcules" a thousand times smaller than the smallest organisms he had ever seen. He observed these creatures living everywhere from the canals in his town to the plaque in his mouth. In the years that followed, legions of scientists would go from doubting the existence of these tiny creatures to recasting them as nothing more than carriers of death and disease.

Ed Yong is not exactly a trained scientist either. But as far as giving a lay audience an unbiased view of microbial life is concerned, he is something better: a science journalist. Weaving accounts of his visits to zoos, labs, and microbe museums with detailed analyses of microbial life, Yong brings to the forefront a shadow world that only microbiologists are really familiar with. The accredited zoologist goes on a mission to cast into perspective the wondrous ecosphere of the tiny animalcules that have, for decades, been given a bum rap by scientists and laymen alike.

I Contain Multitudes is a comprehensive 3D look into the origin and evolution of microbial life, its complex relationship with multi-celled organisms today, and the opportunities and risks it poses in the future. Yong looks back to a past where nothing but microorganisms colonized the Earth and to a future where scientists program the genes of gut bacteria so the bacteria can sense and report on the presence of toxins and pathogens and the onset of disease. In between, Yong combs through centuries' worth of research to illustrate the symbiotic relationship microbes have with their hosts and how this relationship is constantly changing. Yong presents narrative after narrative of everything from how a mother's milk is designed to feed the bacteria in a baby's gut to how microbial transplants are helping end the dengue virus in Australia.

Yong brings these narratives to life with excerpts from Leeuwenhoek's journals, about a dozen photos of microbes and their hosts, and candid interviews with the men and women spearheading research into the microbiome. And while the reader is occasionally left dumbfounded by esoteric vocabulary—the key players in the narrative being bacteroidetes like *Algoriphagus machipongonensis*—Yong goes to great lengths to make his writing conversational and digestible.

On their association with dirt and disease, Yong notes that linking microbes to disease is still a challenge because the microbiome, being a diverse ecosystem, is constantly changing, constantly reassigning the functions of microorganisms depending on context and utility. He notes that the function of the immune system is not to eradicate microbes. Rather, the immune system "works like an immunostat" which manages our relationship with the trillions of microorganisms that live inside us.

If his purpose is to give the reader a "grander view of life," he does so spectacularly. Yong reiterates that "no corner of our biology is untouched" by microorganisms—microbes have a say in everything, from the development of our nervous system to the design of our smell and behavior. He describes a symbiosis unlike anything visible in nature, writing of bacteria living within bacteria within bugs, working together with the host to build enzymes so that "one plus one plus one equals one." Yong leaves the reader pondering his diminutiveness in the grand scheme of things.

KEY TAKEAWAYS

Key Takeaway: Every organism is a diverse ecosystem, host to trillions of microorganisms.

Every living organism—from ants and polar bears to elephants and human beings—has a mass of microscopic organisms (including bacteria, fungi, and viruses, collectively called the microbiota or microbiome) living on its surface, in its gut, in its internal organs and, sometimes, inside its cells.

Microbes colonize some organisms while they are still eggs and others when they are born. Organisms take millions of these microbes everywhere they go. Every organ in a complex organism's body has its characteristic ecosystem that plays host to specific microbial species, complete with intricate food webs and natural balances that must be maintained for the system to function properly.

Microbes exist in more numbers than there are stars in the galaxy, occupying every space from ocean floors to clouds. By rough estimations, the human body plays host to about 39 trillion microbial cells. Of the thousands of microbe species living in the human body, fewer than a hundred species cause infectious disease.

Key Takeaway: Single-celled microorganisms developed before any other forms of life on Earth.

For most of planet Earth's 4.5-billion-years' history, microbes were the only living things crawling its surface. These microorganisms changed the course of history by commandeering cycles of carbon, nitrogen and other elements, releasing oxygen as a waste of photosynthesis, enriching soils, and shaping the evolution of animals.

About two billion years ago, two microorganisms with single cells—a bacterium and an archaeon—merged to form eukaryotes. Eukaryotes are complex organisms with cells that have a central nucleus, mitochondria, and an internal skeleton that maintains the organisms' structure. Current theory has it that eukaryotes evolved into multicellular living organisms and became the ancestors of fungus, alga, plants, and animals. Today, microbes and complex organisms coexist harmoniously because they share a common ancestor. They use the same DNA scheme to store and pass information.

Key Takeaway: Microbes influence the evolution and adaptation of complex organisms.

Microbes carry millions of genes, making them masters of rapid evolution and adaptation. They can digest foods and break down toxins; they can even attack and kill other microbes they deem to be dangerous.

Microbes influence everything from how your body organs develop to how you smell, how you behave, and how much fat you store. They provide plants with nutrients and enable animals to break down food. In the absence of microbes, food supply chains would break down within a year, precipitating the extinction of nearly every species.

"*Many conditions, including obesity, asthma, colon cancer, diabetes, and autism, are accompanied by changes in the microbiome, suggesting that these microbes are at the very least a sign of illness, and at most a cause of it*" (p. 19).

Every individual has a distinctive microbiome shaped by foods he has eaten, places he has lived, drugs he has taken, and things he has touched. Every body part, every organ is a distinctive habitat with its own microbes. And every animal species, while not sharing similar microbes, has distinctive microbes only similar in their function.

Key Takeaway: The discovery of microbes is an ongoing process that dates back to the 1670s.

In 1673, Antony Van Leeuwenhoek, a Dutch city official who doubled as a lens maker, used his hand-made microscopes to observe and document thousands of tiny creatures that moved hastily around a water sample he collected from a lake near his town. By setting his single-lensed microscope to 270X magnification, he was the first to observe what would later be categorized as a group of microorganisms known as protozoa. Leeuwenhoek used his microscopes to look into more water samples and described bacteria.

When he studied plaque from his teeth and from the mouths of a few other subjects, he found thousands more of these microorganisms. Curiously, these microorganisms stopped moving when he doused them with vinegar. Until his death in 1723, Leeuwenhoek saw microorganisms as a fascinating curiosity. If he was ever revolted by the thousands of microorganisms he observed living in his body, he never mentioned it.

Before a Viennese doctor hypothesized in 1762 that microorganisms were disease carriers, it was widely accepted that bad air, not organisms invisible to the naked eye, caused disease. It took the work of Louis Pasteur and Robert Koch in the latter half of the nineteenth century—one studying fermentation and decay and the other studying anthrax—to convince skeptics that bacteria, not bad air, was the culprit. In later years, discoveries of bacteria that cause tuberculosis, gonorrhea, plague, and other diseases shaped the view that these microorganisms were nothing more than disease transmitters—a view that persists to date.

In 1888, Martinus Beijerinck, another Dutch microbiologist, helped shaped a new perspective when he found bacteria that turned nitrogen into ammonia for plants. This discovery influenced the birthing of the term "good bacteria." By the early 1900s, scientists were observing and characterizing bacteria in the human gut and in other species of animals. Their findings pushed to mass acceptance the idea of bacteria-host symbiosis, as well as the idea that most bacteria were, in fact, harmless.

In the 1960s, Carl Woese, an American scientist, began working on a new approach that would become the global standard in studying bacteria. His approach involved the analysis of a molecule called 16S rRNA found in all microbes. In 1976, using this approach, he discovered a new class of methanogens that weren't bacteria. He called these organisms archaea. Woese's approach, which identified microorganisms by sequencing their genes, led to the discovery of more than a hundred new species of bacteria.

Key Takeaway: Microbes activate the genes of the host, influence the development of organisms.

The alliances that microorganisms form with their hosts are complex and repeatedly changing, driving the adaptations and evolution of entire species. The Hawaiian bobtail squid, for example, has luminous bacteria on its underside to cancel out moonlight so that predators don't see the squid from below. The *Vibrio fischeri* bacteria, which collect on the mucus on the underside of the squid, switch on genes that produce antimicrobial chemicals. These chemicals not only drive off other microbes, they attract more of the *V. fischeri* bacteria. The bacteria then move inside the squid, closing the passage behind them so the squid isn't colonized by any other microbes. This process matures the squid and its light organ.

Microbes activate genes involved in the development of animal organs. This co-development occurs because microbes were here first—they shaped the evolution and development of living organisms. A fertilized egg, be it of a human or squid, divides and develops from instructions not just from its parent's genes, but from the genes of microbes.

In the absence of microbes, the development of most organisms would be incomplete—animals would die in their infancy or their organs would fail to develop. The squid, for example, loses its luminescence when bred in a germ-free environment. Without the microbe alliance, organisms would only survive in a protected environment because their weak guts and blood vessels would be easily permeable to toxins.

Sea organisms with larvae stages—such as sea urchins, corals, mussels, lobsters, and oysters—attach to bacteria to transform to adults. Without this union, metamorphosis wouldn't occur.

Microbes move on when their work is done. However, in some organisms, such as the flatworm Paracatenula, microbes occupy most of the host's body, providing energy that facilitates, among other abilities, its regeneration. Life-long symbiosis is also common in animals. Microbes have been known to replenish the skin and gut lining, replace worn-out cells, influence development of immune cells, and maintain a constant internal environment. The immune system, which partly controls microbes, is partly controlled by microbes.

"The immune system's main function is to manage our relationships with our resident microbes. It's more about balance and good management than defense and destruction" (p. 91).

Key Takeaway: Microbes are identity shapers.

When a dotted hyena releases a chemical streak from the scent gland in its backside, it leaves a bio-signature unique only to itself. The bacteria in the scent glands produce a distinctive smell which indicates, among other things, the health, age, and fertility of the host. The smell, and in extension, the bacteria, affects the mating behavior and other idiosyncrasies of the animal. The bacteria in the urine of other animals—and in human armpits—leave a similar bio-signature.

Microbes don't just report on the condition of their host; they affect its behavior as well. A change in the microbiome of mice has been shown to change chemicals in its brain, its personality, and its susceptibility to mental illnesses. Timid mice have been emboldened when their guts were colonized with microbes from bold mice. Scientists have had some success in using probiotics to reduce symptoms of anxiety and depression, and there is already potential for other mental issues.

Key Takeaway: There are no good or bad microbes; microbes are like tools that change function depending on context.

Wolbachia pipientis, a bacterium that infects 40 percent of arthropods insects, is one of the most successful bacteria on Earth. Part of the reason it has been so successful is because it manipulates the sex lives of its hosts to ensure its own survival. It kills male hosts in butterflies, transmutes males into females in woodlice, and restructures female wasps so that they reproduce asexually. The bacterium is passed on through eggs, not sperms, so it disposes of male hosts. In the species affected by Wolbachia, there is a markedly disproportionate population of females and males. Yet Wolbachia is not entirely a manipulation machine. It makes B-vitamins for bed bugs, protects mosquitoes and flies from viruses, and is critical to the development of nematode worms.

Wolbachia reflects the double personalities of bacteria: some are as much allies as they are pathogens. Beneficial microbes can create weaknesses that pathogens use to launch attack. The same strain of *Helicobacter pylori* that protects against esophageal cancer causes stomach cancer and ulcers. Essential microbes in aphids release molecules that attract predators. The microbes that release molecules that attract malaria-carrying mosquitoes to some people are the same microbes that release molecules that put off the same mosquitoes in other people.

Harmless bacteria can be life-threatening if they end up in the wrong part of the body. Beneficial gut bacteria, for example, can cause a host of diseases if they pass into the bloodstream and are carried to other organs.

Key Takeaway: The relationship between microbes and their hosts, though symbiotic, is rife with conflict.

While the relationship between microbes and hosts is symbiotic and important, it is anything but harmonious. Although the host feeds, houses, and warms microbes, they can stop performing a crucial role to save on energy. Pathogens may even draw from the energy supplied by the host to launch more attacks and multiply. At any given time, there's a constant battle to balance conflicting interests. The body uses temperature, acidity, oxygen levels, and other internal regulatory mechanisms to restrain pathogens and free riders and dictate where strains of microbes live.

Some mechanisms that have evolved over time, such as the underside vaults of the bobtail squid, keep beneficial microbes where they need to be so they don't turn into threats. Some insects have specialized cells called bacteriocytes to house bacteria so they don't spread to other tissue and wreak havoc on the immune system. They use these cells to regulate the movement of nutrients, stave off unruly bacteria, or feed beneficial bacteria toxic enzymes when their work is done.

The human gut has an outer layer of mucus, where microbes live, and an inner layer, beneath which there are epithelial cells. These cells spray antimicrobial peptides to any microbes that attempt to cross the inner layer and into the bloodstream. Bacterial molecules may stimulate the gut to create more mucus to strengthen the gut's defense and create a better niche for microbes.

Key Takeaway: Microbes are at the heart of the health and extinction of corals reefs.

About a third of corals—which have been building reefs for hundreds of millions of years—face extinction today. As human activity raises levels of carbon dioxide in the atmosphere, oceans get warmer, driving away the algae that live in and provide reefs with nutrient.

Carbon dioxide doesn't just raise atmospheric temperatures; it acidifies oceans, corrodes the limestone that makes up corals, and, consequently, leaves reefs homeless and defenseless.

A dense network of microbes on the surface of the corals creates a blockade that keeps out pathogens. If these microbes are unsettled, either by warming or acidifying waters, they leave the corals vulnerable to several diseases, which is what is driving them to extinction.

Key Takeaway: The weight of organisms is driven by a combination of microbes and diet.

Microbiologists have observed that the groups of microbes that colonize the guts of obese people and mice are different from those that colonize their lean counterparts. Microbes from obese mice transplanted into the guts of normal mice have caused as much as 47 percent fat gain. Obese mice fed *Akkermansia muciniphila*, the gut bacteria that are 3,000 times more common in lean mice than in fat mice, lost weight and recorded reduced signs of type 2 diabetes.

These findings come with one caveat: the lifestyle of the host has more influence on its weight than the presence of the right microbes. Communities of lean microbes cannot flourish in an unhealthy environment such as one created by a host subsisting on a diet of fatty, low-fiber foods.

The presence (and absence) of groups of microbes influence not just weight, but general health as well. In Western countries, the risk of allergic and inflammatory diseases is growing because urbanization (and the concomitant ultra-sanitization) has been reducing the range of microbes people are exposed to. Dust microbes fed to mice in labs have been shown to reduce their sensitivity to allergens.

Caesarean section babies not colonized by the beneficial vaginal microbes of their mothers have a higher risk of developing allergies, asthma, and even obesity than their traditionally delivered counterparts. If these babies are bottle-fed, the growth of microbes that feed on sugars in breast milk is suppressed, exacerbating these health problems.

Key Takeaway: Antibiotic overuse is destroying natural microbes, creating the possibility of an apocalyptic "antibiotic winter."

Antibiotics kill both harmful and beneficial bacteria. Some bacteria disappear after a course of antibiotics. Some resurface, but not in their original state. Disappearing microbes open pathways to disease because they let down the defenses put up to invasive pathogens. Pathogens assume the spaces created by the disappearing bacteria and feed on the nutrients left. Antibiotics, by weakening and eliminating the gut's native microbiome, create opportunities for pathogens to exploit.

Today, Triclosan and other antibacterial chemicals are present in a wide range of consumer products—from cosmetics and toothpastes to toys and clothes. As bacteria are masters of adaptation, the overuse of antibiotics and of these chemicals is likely to herald a nightmarish future where antibiotics are ineffective.

Studies have already demonstrated that a low diversity of microbes corresponds with incidence of obesity, inflammation, and metabolic problems. However, studies that link microbiome diversity and disease are mostly correlational; further research is still needed to prove a causal relationship. Still, antibiotics should be used sparingly.

Key Takeaway: Microbes and complex organisms have coexisted from the beginning of time, shaping each other's progress.

It's possible that before they colonized hosts, microbes lived freely in the environment, piggybacking on the bodies of animals to get to new ecosystems.

Microbes, as they evolved, provided carrier animals with nutrients and other benefits and moved into their cells. These early microbes were passed around when hosts mated, shared fluids, or simply got together. As they were passed to the offspring, the microbes lost the genes they needed to survive in the open and became a permanent part of the host. Hosts themselves evolved mechanisms to protect beneficial bacteria.

In humans, the first (of lifelong) contact with bacteria is in the birth canal. Many animals—rats and gorillas included—eat each other's feces to replenish their supply of gut bacteria, which aids food digestion. It's possible that some animals became social and began to live in large groups not just to hunt or to put up collective defense, but to pass around beneficial microbes.

Key Takeaway: Symbiosis can influence evolution and the emergence of new species.

Microbe hosts are selective about the microbes they let in, as are microbes about the hosts they invade. Hosts, through their distinct genes, set conditions that only allow some microbes to thrive. Microbes, on their part, only colonize specific symbionts. They either die in or adapt to an unfamiliar environment. Hosts and microbes adapt to each other over time and evolve as one organism.

Microbes can influence the creation of a new species if animals of the same species are separated by physical obstacles or other barriers that prevent mating. Different diets and habits affect the microbiome, which affects the smell of the animals, which affects their sexual preferences, which isolates groups of the same animals. Essentially, different groups of microbes in the same animal can create an evolutionary rift.

Key Takeaway: Microbes steer the success of species.

Microbes can give their hosts new abilities that enable them to eat previously indigestible foods and thrive where they'd fail as a species. Aphid microbes, for example, supplement the bug with vital amino acids not available in the phloem sap that aphids feed on. Some bugs that eat whole plant cells have discarded their symbionts because they get enough amino acids from their food. At least 10 percent of insects depend on microbes to provide amino acids, sterols, and vitamins of which their diets are deficient.

A mile and half down the ocean around Galapagos Islands, scientists have found giant worms with no mouth or gut. Because there's no solar energy this deep in the ocean, bacteria in the worms oxidize sulphides in the rocks and use the energy released to make food for the worms. Shrimp, clams, and a variety of animals in deep oceans depend on bacteria for practically everything.

Even in mammals, bacteria supply enzymes that steer the success of entire species. Herbivores have the largest diversity of microbes because the complex carbohydrates in plants can only be broken down by bacteria enzymes. Carnivores have the least diversity, and omnivores are somewhere in between. Bacteria provide as much as 70 percent of energy intake in grazing animals and only about 10 percent in humans. Mammals, the first of which were carnivores, diversified and spread by shifting to eating plants, which were in abundant supply. Microbes, by supplying enzymes that enabled this shift, drove the success of mammals.

"In other words, microbes shaped the evolution of the mammalian gut, and the shape of the mammalian gut influenced the evolution of microbes" (p. 178).

Bacteria also steers the success of some animals by neutralizing toxins in the plants in their environment.

Animals with the right bacteria, such as desert woodrats, can subsist on creosote—a toxic plant—which kills lab mice and other rodents not colonized by the bacteria. When woodrats are fed antibiotics, they are less tolerant of the toxin in creosote. Reindeer feed on lichens, which are full of the poisonous usnic acid, because their gut microbes neutralize the acid.

Key Takeaway: Partnerships with microbes enable animals to speed up their evolution.

Horizontal gene transfers enable bacteria to borrow superior genes from their neighbors as easily as people borrow phone numbers. These transfers enable bacteria to cope in unfriendly environments. Without this capability, bacteria would have to wait around for millennia for mutations to foster adaptations. Bacteria can borrow from their neighbors traits that enable them to resist antibiotics and break down new sources of energy. When animals can pick up microbes with the right adaptations, they hasten adaptation to their own environmental challenges.

Bacteria genes aren't just traded between neighbors; they also make their way into the genome of the host. The coffee berry borer beetle, for example, has bacterial genes in its genome that enable it to digest the carbs in coffee beans.

Bacteria that develop genes to fight off other bacteria pass the antibiotic genes to their host, which they use for defense—as observed in ticks, sea slugs, and scorpions. Some symbionts change the color of aphids from red to green so they can adapt to new environments.

"(Bacteria) are metabolic wizards that can digest everything from uranium to crude oil. They are expert pharmacologists that excel at making chemicals that kill each other. If you want to defend yourself from another creature or eat a new source of food, there's almost certainly a microbe that already has the right tools for the job" (p. 207).

Key Takeaway: Probiotics work better in a supportive gut environment.

Microbes are not communities of disease-carrying soldiers. The microbiome is more like a garden with some weeds. The weeds need to be pruned, but the garden needs to be nurtured too.

Probiotics add beneficial microbes to the body. These microbes can reduce the risk of diarrhea and shorten bouts of the condition. There's little evidence, however, that probiotics can help people with diabetes, allergies, or other microbe-related conditions.

Yoghurt is one of the most accessible sources of probiotics, but its value is severely limited. Because the probiotics in yoghurt are produced from industrial cultures, the bacteria chosen are the ones easiest to grow, not necessarily the most beneficial. Studies have shown that the single strains of bacteria in yoghurt don't colonize or alter the microbiome of the adult gut. In 2014, the EU banned the inclusion of the word 'probiotics' in the packaging and advertising of foods because food products with probiotics didn't confer the health benefits they implied.

Probiotics colonize guts most effectively when they find it preloaded with their favorite food. The oxalobacter microbe feeds on and destroys oxalate, the chemical that causes kidney stones. Patients with kidney stones can take the oxalobacter probiotic to remedy their condition, but if they go on an oxalate-free diet, they starve the bacterium and render it ineffective.

Bacteria, especially those in probiotics, need support to work. Probiotics could adjust the gut's microbiome and be more effective if they were packed with a community of microbes rather than with single strains of bacteria. For people with the bacterial infection known as C-diff, faecal transplants work better than antibiotics because they recolonize the gut with an entire community of beneficial bacteria.

Key Takeaway: Sterilization undermines a diverse microbiome and creates opportunities for pathogens to flourish.

Despite the best sterilization efforts, between 5 and 10 percent of people who check into healthcare institutions in the developing world will pick up infections there. It's possible that while sterilization techniques have helped save countless lives, they have created—by destroying harmless bacteria—spaces for pathogens to flourish. Sanitation hasn't just undermined microbe diversity; it has eliminated the microbes that keep pathogens in check. Healthcare institutions should be looking to repopulate rooms with benign microbes instead of destroying them.

"...sterility is a curse not a goal, and a diverse ecosystem is better than an impoverished one. These principles are the same whether we're talking about a human intestine or an aquarium tank – or even a hospital room" (p. 255).

ABOUT THE AUTHOR

Ed Soon-Weng Yong is a British science journalist and a pop science blogger. Born in 1981, Yong acquired his Bachelor and Master of Arts degrees in Natural Sciences from the University of Cambridge in 2002. He has been working with *The Atlantic* since 2015.

Yong has won numerous awards for his work, including the National Academies Communication Award in 2010 and Stephen White Award in 2012. In 2012, his blog, *Not Exactly Rocket Science*, was recognized as the best science blog by the Association of British Science Writers. *I Contain Multitudes*, which was published in September 2016, is his first book.

THE END

If you enjoyed this analysis, please leave an honest review on Amazon.com…it'd mean a lot to us.

If you haven't already, we encourage you to purchase a copy of the original book.

Made in United States
North Haven, CT
04 October 2022

24990856R00017